Chakras

Promoting The Restoration And Purification Of Your Third Eye Chakra Through Sleep Meditation To Enhance Your Consciousness

(The Definitive Manual On Achieving Chakra Equilibrium)

Gilberto Foglia

TABLE OF CONTENT

The Mechanisms of Energy Chakra Healing 1

Gaining insight into your Chakras and nurturing your vitality. 13

Yoga Asanas for Enhancing the Muladhara Chakra 43

The Sacral Chakra 72

Chakras and Their Interaction with the Physical Body 81

Swadhisthana, the Sacral 110

Lifting the Veil 127

Healing the Sixth Chakra 144

Techniques for Restoring Balance 171

The Mechanisms of Energy Chakra Healing

Chakras are subtle energy vortices located along the spinal column. They oversee and manage all aspects of life. The chakras have been extensively documented in various ancient texts, particularly in the realm of yoga philosophy. Traditionally, the majority of teachings recognize seven prominent chakras, while certain systems acknowledge the existence of additional minor chakras.

The imbalance of specific chakras can have profound effects on various aspects of life, encompassing physical well-being, financial matters, social relationships, emotions, communication, and general feelings of volatility. The purpose of this section is not to delve deeply into the meaning of the chakras, as there is already a wealth of information available on the subject.

There exist a plethora of methods to facilitate the clarity, invigoration, and harmonization of the chakras. There exists a range of contemplative techniques, rituals, and various methods one may engage in to restore the optimal functioning of the chakras. Distant chakra healing and balancing can be highly effective for promoting chakra healing. This approach may seem unconventional to many individuals; however, it has been employed in the Far East for an extended period of time, and now alternative contemporary methodologies have emerged. A growing population has increasingly turned towards alternative forms of healing, such as remote chakra healing, as a means to enhance their well-being and overall health.

Qigong energy healing employs a rigorous approach to promote equilibrium, cleanse, realign, and restore the chakras. Distant Qigong energy healing has proven to be useful for addressing a range of psychological, physiological, and intense conditions in both Eastern and Western societies. It has also demonstrated significant efficacy in the realm of chakra healing. In what way can remote Qigong energy healing have a positive impact on the chakras and other energy pathways? The efficacy of remote energy healing has been subject to experimental investigation in various institutions, such as the California Pacific Medical Center in Northern California and The Institute of Noetic Sciences, for instance.

A rigorous double-blind study conducted by cardiologist Robert Bryd, encompassing approximately 400 patients, established that individuals who were prayed for exhibited more favorable outcomes compared to those who did not receive such intervention. Quantum Physics may provide insights into the mechanisms underlying the efficacy of remote or distant healing.

In the 1980s, a group of researchers led by Alain Aspect at the University of Paris unveiled a remarkable revelation, which could be considered one of the most significant discoveries in contemporary science. In certain specific circumstances, it has been ascertained that certain subatomic particles possess the ability to promptly engage in discourse with one another, irrespective of the considerable distances that separate them. The geographic distance between them did not affect the outcome. In 1997, Nicolas Gisan replicated these findings and postulated that certain particles appeared to be shared at an astonishing velocity exceeding that of light by a multiple of three. These outcomes may provide insights into the mechanisms underlying the efficacy of distance healing.

Renowned quantum physicist David Bohm, in his analysis, infers that the persistence of contact between subatomic particles, even across vast distances that defy comprehension, is not attributable to the exchange of some mysterious signal back and forth. Rather, he posits that the apparent separation of the particles is illusory. Bohm postulates that on a deeper stratum of existence, particles are not discrete entities but rather manifestations of a shared fundamental essence, whereby the entirety of the universe is intricately interconnected without limits.

Several scholars presently acknowledge the longstanding wisdom of mystics across different cultures who have posited for millennia that we are not merely isolated entities, but fundamentally interlinked on a spiritual level.

The exchange of energy in distance healing occurs across vast distances due to the interconnectedness of all individuals involved. It is inconsequential whether the power transmission originates from a different city or even from a distant location around the globe than the intended recipient, as the effect remains negligible.

Sacral Chakra - To Experience Sensations

The chakra known as "Svadhisthana," denoting a personal abode or "the abode of the self," is also commonly referred to as the sacral chakra. It serves as the focal point for your sensory experiences, sentiments, and affective responses. The sacral chakra pertains to matters of sexuality, overall well-being, sensuality, pleasure, fertility, the creative life force, and a sense of abundance. This particular chakra pertains to various aspects of one's identity and individuality, while also fostering personal growth and advancement. It represents an avenue for cultivating adaptability in one's life, enabling the capacity to embrace and connect with others and the surrounding environment. It provides a source of inspiration, fostering creative vitality and prompting one to indulge in the delights of existence.

The sacral chakra is intricately linked to the element of water. It is intricately linked to the dynamics and progression of our cognitive processes and affective states. Typically situated in the central region of the lower abdomen, approximately three inches beneath the naval.

The sacral chakra is typically signified by a hue of orange that possesses a slight translucency. It bears an emblem comprising a circular shape with six petals and a crescent-shaped celestial body. The circular symbol embodies the essence of water, while the lunar symbol signifies the intricate interplay between water's energy and the celestial body. The moon symbol is additionally linked to the feminine menstrual cycle due to its comparable duration and the connection between the chakra and the processes of sexual organs and reproduction.

This subsequent energy center is motivated by the pursuit of sensory gratification. It serves as a catalyst for us to derive pleasure from the intricacies of life through our sensory perceptions. When we activate our sacral chakra, we experience heightened sensitivity to our immediate environment. It serves as the foundation for our notion of well-being, rendering it indispensable.

In order to restore equilibrium to the sacral chakra, it is imperative that we release any lingering feelings of guilt or blame that reside within us, thus facilitating the activation of the sacral chakra. It is imperative that we grant ourselves forgiveness for our perceived errors, recognizing that the knowledge we have gained from these experiences has fostered greater resilience and wisdom, thereby attaining a state that could be defined as perfection.

The Sacral Chakra and Complementary Therapies

Color: Orange

Element: Water

Position: Directly beneath the navel, spanning a distance of two inches towards the midline

Psychological Disorders resulting from Obstructions: Substance Dependence, Hostility, Envy, Chronic unease, decreased libido, remorse, stifled artistic expression

Physical Afflictions due to Obstructions: Discomfort in the back region, intense menstrual cramps, urinary or renal complications, and issues related to the prostate gland.

Healing through the use of crystals includes varieties such as tiger's eye, silver quartz, rainbow fluorite, moonstone, golden topaz, Dalmatian jasper, citrine, carnelian, aventurine, coral, and fire opal.

The Therapeutic Potential of Herbal Remedies: Examining the Benefits of Nettle, Parsley, and Yarrow

Healing through the application of Bach Flower Therapy utilizing the essences of Oak, Pine, and Olive

Healing through the Utilization of Essential Oils: The Therapeutic Benefits of Myrrh, Orange, Pepper, Sandalwood, and Vanilla

"Utilizing the Power of Sound for Healing: Enchant the Omnipotent Seed Sound - "VAM"

Healing through Positive Declarations: "I wholeheartedly embrace the pleasures of life" "I gratefully invite joy into my existence as I embark on new endeavors" "I hold deep appreciation for my physical vessel" "I am a sentient entity, fully attuned to my senses

Stimulating the Sacral Chakra: Engage with water - Engage in a bathing or swimming activity. Engage in artistic endeavors such as painting or culinary activities to stimulate your creativity. Engaging in dance forms such as belly dancing, salsa, and tango invigorate the sacral chakra.

Meditative/Yogic Posture: Baddha Konasana/Butterfly Pose

Gaining insight into your Chakras and nurturing your vitality.

Recognizing that all elements in one's surroundings possess energy is the preliminary stage in comprehending the workings of the cosmos. In accordance with the elegant explanations offered by physics, it can be stated that matter is subject to an immutable law wherein it is not susceptible to creation or annihilation, but rather experiences a perpetual transmutation between various states. Isn't it astonishing that this was a concept that our ancestors were familiar with a mere 6000 years ago? Through their unassisted perception, they were able to ascertain the awe-inspiring nature of the universe, as well as the veracity that energy permeates our surroundings, even in the absence of microscopic instruments. Analogizing each chakra to a wheel, enabling the transmission of energy throughout our beings, thereby establishing alignment with the cosmic realm and the wisdom accumulated over centuries that permeates our existence.

The practice of utilizing the chakras revolves around the essential task of maintaining equilibrium among each individual chakra, thus ensuring harmonious energy circulation throughout the entirety of the body. To effectively utilize the entirety of the energy, it is essential to possess the necessary internal equilibrium, ensuring the proper alignment and stability of all chakras, without any disarray or disturbances. In the system, one can observe numerous varieties of chakras, and it is imperative to acquire the knowledge and skill to ensure their harmonious satisfaction, while avoiding any deviations that may induce imbalance. There exists a wide array of yoga postures that facilitate the harmonious alignment of your bodily elements.

The initial chakra is referred to as the root chakra, and it serves as the foundation, crucially contributing to both personal accomplishment and the capacity to endure. When experiencing imbalances in this specific energy center, individuals may notice an unintended increase in body weight that necessitates addressing the underlying concerns affecting their physical well-being. By prioritizing inner equilibrium and gaining access to optimal equilibrium throughout the body, you will acquire the means to effectively address this obesity issue, leading to a more harmonious alignment with the various forces in your life.

The Sacral Chakra oversees numerous faculties that enable individuals to effectively address their overall sense of well-being. Especially in regards to maintaining homeostasis and acknowledging the plentiful blessings inherent in your daily existence, all of this is predominantly governed by this chakra, enabling you to achieve harmonious equilibrium with the external world. Furthermore, you will also achieve equilibrium with your bodily requirements, encompassing various physiological desires. When an individual experiences an imbalance with this particular chakra, it frequently manifests as promiscuity and an array of excessive sexual concerns. Frequently, this implies that the individual will display diverse behaviors, leading to sexual concerns that will manifest in their lives.

The Solar Plexus Chakra serves as the dwelling place of an individual's intrinsic value, alongside their assurance and self-regard. The occurrence of imbalance in this region contributes to a propensity for excessive food consumption and a persistent lack of self-esteem among individuals. By restoring equilibrium to the other chakras through its reinstatement into stasis, one can effectively introduce an overall state of harmony and vitality to the entire physical being. There are numerous individuals who remain unaware of their inherent worth until they regain equilibrium within themselves.

The Heart Chakra, situated at the center of the chest, governs one's inner serenity, compassionate affection, and profound delight. In the event of an imbalance within this chakra, one may experience a state of imbalance, characterized by incessantly seeking new relationships and pursuing new love interests. Occasionally, when faced with a pressing situation, an individual who is already committed can find themselves drawn into an act of betrayal. It is of utmost significance to ensure that one possesses the epitome of excellence in every circumstance, alongside achieving optimal equilibrium in each of their chakras.

The Throat Chakra is the chakra that symbolizes various aspects of communication and the articulation of emotions. When one's chakra becomes imbalanced, communicating genuine emotions can become exceptionally challenging. Moreover, expressing complete honesty may prove to be arduous in certain instances.

The Third Eye Chakra bestows upon individuals the capacity to make sound judgments, possess mental clarity, and acquire wisdom. Due to all of these aforementioned factors, when an individual experiences an inability to engage in clear thinking and maintain mental clarity, it is possible that the root cause lies in an obstruction of the third eye chakra. It is highly advisable to invest considerable effort in strategizing and contemplation towards the enhancement of your equilibrium, along with thorough consideration of the manifold elements in your surroundings, thereby facilitating a heightened ability to concentrate.

The Crown Chakra is the chakra responsible for symbolizing your manifestation of alignment with the vast expanse of the cosmos, as well as your inherent capacity for experiencing absolute transcendental contentment. When one establishes a suitable connection with everything within their environment, they will perceive their capacity to attain universal access to all essential elements.

The complete harmonization of every chakra enables individuals to establish a profound connection with their inner energies and comprehend the potency and essence of the Earth and their environment. In the absence of a suitable symbiosis with the cosmos, individuals may experience a profound sense of seclusion, frigidity, and disassociation. Hence, it is imperative, should we aspire to unlock our utmost capabilities, to embark on a journey of self-discovery, thereby enabling us to align harmoniously with our surroundings.

The Chakra associated with the forehead, also known as the Third Eye Chakra or the Brow Chakra.

The third eye chakra, which is the sixth in the sequence of the body's chakras, is renowned for its correlation with perception and mental imagery. Positioned a notch above the ocular region on the frontal part of the cranium, the third eye chakra pertains to the inclination to ponder upon the spiritual essence of one's existence. It denotes cognition and understanding, introspective sight, sagacity and intuitive discernment. Another intriguing aspect to comprehend regarding this particular chakra is the comprehensive storage it harbors, housing not only the aspirations encompassing this current existence, but also encompassing the memories encapsulating myriad prior life cycles. Consequently, obstruction or disruption in this energy center could result in impaired memory function, diminished ability to anticipate future events, and persistent feelings of despondency.

The somatic regulation of this chakra encompasses the ocular faculties, visual perception, the olfactory senses, the neural network, and the central nervous system. Consequently, any impairment or deficiency in the functioning of this particular chakra will result in distinct physical manifestations within one or multiple regions of the body. Conversely, in the presence of equilibrium and activation of the sixth chakra, one would experience a heightened sense of dominion over their existence, enabling them to summon the audacity to pursue their desires without hesitation.

Individuals with an active sixth chakra will experience a profound sense of confidence and self-assurance, enhancing their belief in their own abilities and attributes. An additional consequence arising from this phenomenon is that a diminished energy flow through the center of consciousness located within your brow chakra may engender a state of distorted perception, leading to various psychological manifestations such as spiritual fatigue and melancholy.

Additionally, a deficient functioning of the sixth chakra can induce disarray, trepidation, and a general indifference towards the emotional well-being of those in your vicinity. An excess amount of energy present in this particular area is also unfavorable for maintaining a harmonious balance in your chakras. It results in cognitive disarray, diminished attention span, and a pervasive feeling of persistent despair within the individual in question. Therefore, it is imperative for an optimal state to be achieved through the attainment of equilibrium in the flow of energy within the sixth sense. In the event of an insufficiently functioning sixth chakra, it is advisable to recline on a level surface and position a crystal atop the third eye. Additionally, it is recommended to employ the practice of visualizing either an indigo light or an indigo flame during the meditation process. This technique has proven to be markedly efficacious in rectifying any imbalances within the third eye chakra and reinstating its harmonious functioning.

The Crown Chakra

Situated in the cranial region or atop the cranium, the crown chakra is symbolized by the hue of violet. This particular chakra possesses a profound basis in spiritual wisdom, thereby establishing a strong affiliation with matters of spirituality. It serves to enhance our understanding of celestial phenomena, bolster our spiritual resolve, provide guidance, and foster idealistic perspectives in our interconnectedness with the universe. The effective functioning of the crown chakra additionally fosters impartiality towards individuals encountered, along with facilitating a deep connection to oneself and the world, thereby promoting a sense of belonging. The physiological impact of the crown chakra is primarily manifested within the cerebral region and the central nervous system.

When a state of equilibrium is achieved in the crown chakra, one is able to relinquish desires rooted in self-centeredness and materialistic pursuits. However, the absence of such balance results in the development of an ego-driven persona, whose primary objective in life revolves around gratifying one's own ego. Additionally, it engenders a deficit in one's self-assurance and instills feelings of apprehension and unease. The adverse consequences of the crown chakra on the physical body can manifest as indifference and impairment in the acquisition and retention of knowledge acquired over time. Additional physiological manifestations of the crown chakra can encompass symptoms such as a throbbing sensation in the head, disruptions in the immune system, as well as heightened feelings of unease and distress.

An excessively active crown chakra can lead to a compulsion towards spirituality, resulting in the neglect of one's physical well-being. Consequently, an excessively stimulated crown chakra hinders the activity of the remaining chakras in your body. Consequently, it is imperative to establish a harmonious equilibrium between your crown chakra and the remaining chakras within your body to fully embrace a life of utmost fulfillment. If you are experiencing an insufficiency in the functioning of your crown chakra, it is imperative to regularly engage in the practice of meditation in order to establish a connection with your spiritual essence, thus facilitating the restoration of equilibrium within the crown chakra.

Consider introspecting on whether the chosen course aligns aptly with your pursuits. Through gradual and methodical progression, coupled with diligent training, one would successfully attain harmonious equilibrium within the crown chakra.

Crystals for Enhancing the Third Eye Chakra

When the alignment of your Third Eye is disrupted, you will experience a tendency to close yourself off from novel concepts, distrust others, and witness a disarray in your intuitive faculties.

The Third Eye Chakra can be supported in its stabilization by employing chakra stones such as Amethyst, Fluorite, Azurite, Blue Aventurine, Lapis Lazuli, Lolite, Celestite, Angelite, and Sugilite.

When your Third Eye is harmonized, you will experience heightened intuition, enhanced mental clarity, and an increased capacity to effectively address and overcome challenges and difficulties.

Crystalline Gemstones designed to balance the Crown Chakra

An individual's experience of stress and cognitive impairment may be attributed to the lack of stability in their Crown Chakra. You are likely to experience a sense of disorientation, with a pervasive sense of uncertainty overshadowing various facets of your life. You will experience a profound sense of aimlessness and lack of purpose in your life.

The subsequent assortment of chakra stones will provide considerable assistance, encompassing White Topaz, Moonstone, Blue Opal, Amethyst, Selenite, Blue Sapphire, White Calcite, and Clear Quartz.

To facilitate the restoration and harmonization of your Crown Chakras, it is recommended to utilize the aforementioned stones by gently placing them upon the crown of your head while focusing your thoughts upon the radiance of violet or white luminosity. Your existence will abound with illumination and meaning. Furthermore, you will gain a beneficial outlook even in the face of setbacks, enabling you to effectively pursue and accomplish your aspirations in life.

How to Discern the Activation of Your Chakras

All of our thoughts, sentiments, emotions, and encounters pertain to our energy system and chakras. It is crucial to devote careful consideration to the various facets of our existence in order to discern the moments when our chakras are being activated, as well as to recognize any instances of imbalance or blockage within them, given that chakras are consistently employed by us. For example, in the event that I exhibit controlling tendencies while also displaying high levels of energy and motivation, it would suggest an imbalance in my chakras that requires attention and rectification in order to achieve stability within them. Please find a succinct overview below elucidating the conduct of each chakra during its state of openness:

Comprehending the Fundamentals of the First Chakra-Root

Your physiological well-being will be in good condition, ensuring a fundamental sense of protection and stability, as well as fostering a sense of being firmly anchored. You can expect the promotion of optimal foot and bone health, maintenance of desirable weight, support for proper functioning of adrenal glands, colon health, and efficient elimination. Your capacity to efficiently carry out everyday tasks will be exceptional.

Comprehending the Function of the Second Chakra-Sacral Chakra

"You will experience equitable sexual fulfillment, robust vitality, receptiveness to adaptation, sound urinary and reproductive functionality." You will also encounter a sense of delight, and your second chakra will be in balance, neither excessively active nor inactive.

Gaining Insight into the Third Chakra: Solar Plexus

When one's third chakra is unblocked, they will possess the capacity to attain their objectives within the material realm. You will develop a sense of personal value. The individual is expected to possess a well-functioning immune system, digestive system, musculoskeletal system, and adrenal glands. You will not encounter significant allergic reactions.

Comprehending the Unblocking of the Fourth Chakra: An Exploration of the Heart

When this chakra is fully activated, you will exhibit a genuine sense of empathy and compassion towards others. Additionally, you will have the capacity to nurture robust interpersonal connections, experience a profound sense of emotional fulfillment, establish a profound link with the natural world, and cultivate a disposition of forgiveness towards others. You are encouraged to demonstrate benevolence towards oneself and others. You will develop robust pulmonary function, dexterous extremities, proficient upper appendages, resilient thymus gland, and a well-functioning cardiovascular system.

Gaining Insight into the Fifth Chakra - Throat

When this chakra is activated, you will possess the capacity to articulate your ideas and personal convictions. You will have the ability to engage in auditory perception, exercise creative self-expression, maintain oral and aural health, support the wellbeing of your neck, shoulders, sinuses, nose, and vocal apparatus.

Comprehending the Sixth Chakra-The Third Eye

You shall possess cognitive prowess complemented by other cognitive faculties such as strong concentration, discernment, exceptional recall, intuitive abilities, and a capacity for holistic understanding. Moreover, you shall enjoy optimal ocular health, visual acuity, well-functioning hypothalamus, and pituitary gland.

Comprehending the Optimal State of the Seventh Chakra - Crown

If one's seventh chakra is fully activated, an individual will experience an enhanced perception of interconnectedness with a higher purpose and an increased sense of inner strength. This heightened state of being will bring about a greater reservoir of wisdom, serenity, an expanded consciousness, a genuine acceptance of others, and a steadfast mental equilibrium. You shall possess a well-functioning pineal gland and cerebral cortex, contributing to your overall good health.

Yoga Asanas for Balancing the Muladhara Chakra

To attain equilibrium in your root chakra, it is necessary to experience complete bodily comfort. Please adopt a relaxed posture, ideally with your legs crossed and hands placed gently on top of each knee, while holding the Mundra associated with the Muladhara. A Mundra is a manual gesture employed in yoga for the purpose of highlighting and stimulating the energies of a specific grouping of energy situated along the spinal column or chakra system. The Mundra corresponding to the root chakra entails bringing together the thumb and index finger to form the universally recognized gesture of "OK." While assuming this posture, direct your attention towards the auditory experience of your respiration during inhalation and exhalation. Direct your attention solely to the sound of your breath, and over time, your mind will progressively experience a reduction in the number of thoughts, ultimately achieving a state of thoughtlessness.

The objective of meditation is to achieve a state of complete absence of thoughts. The fundamental resonance of the Muladhara chakra is manifested as the sound 'lum.' Remaining in the aforementioned posture, emanate auditory vibrations from the abdomen, expelling them through the oral cavity. The primary phonetic element is articulated as 'lung.' Sustain the phoneme while exhaling fully and proceed with repetition. In the process of undertaking this activity, endeavor to direct the energy residing within your physical being towards the region of your pelvis. Consistently contemplate subjects pertaining to the terrestrial realm, such as the natural world, sustenance, progeny, or dwelling.

In order to concentrate the energy within a specific region of your body, envision the resonance generated by your vocal cords and direct it towards your pelvic region. Engage in this practice consistently for approximately one minute each day, and gradually, you will experience a sensation in your pelvic region while engaging in mindful meditation. This indicates that you are effectively directing energy towards your Muladhara, leading to its gradual expansion and the subsequent release of Kundalini energy throughout your entire being.

The subsequent posture that can be assumed to facilitate the restoration of equilibrium to the root chakra is the child pose. Maintain the seated posture with crossed legs, and proceed to incline your upper body forward, extending your arms as far as feasible while directing your gaze towards the floor. Enable your body to unwind and place your forehead gently on the floor. Extend your arms forward and maintain contact of your hands with the floor. Try to imagine yourself sinking deep into the earth, becoming one with the ground beneath you. This will facilitate the awakening and stimulation of the root chakra residing within your being.

An additional asana that can be assumed is the posture known as the garland pose. It necessitates assuming a crouched posture, with your weight on your haunches. Preserve a tightly aligned stance by ensuring minimal distance between your feet, all the while maintaining equilibrium, and widen the positioning of your thighs. Maintaining an upright posture, exert pressure with your elbows against your inner thigh and join your palms in unison. Once more, envision the gradual descent of your feet into the soil, establishing a profound connection as roots firmly anchor and stabilize you within the depths of the earth.

To initiate the standing forward bend, assume an upright stance. During the expiration phase, proceed to lean forward and endeavor to establish contact between your hands and toes by means of bending. Exert downward pressure with your feet against the ground while clasping each elbow with your hands. When executing the inhalation, elevate your torso in a slight upward movement and subsequently exhale, gradually lowering it towards the ground. Please perform these steps for a few respiratory cycles. In this posture, it is essential to surrender to the force of gravity and allow it to draw your body nearer to the surface of the earth.

The mountain pose is exceedingly uncomplicated. Assume a posture in which your feet are positioned in close proximity, your arms are held adjacent to your body, maintaining an upright and straight back, while ensuring tension in your legs. Maintain an erect posture and visualize your feet extending roots that penetrate the ground while engaging in inhalation and exhalation.

The next pose in the sequence aims to facilitate the opening of your root chakra. In this role, proceed by taking a significant stride forward and flexing your leading knee to achieve a 90-degree angle. Ensure that your back leg remains fully extended, exerting pressure on your toes to establish a solid foundation upon shifting your weight onto your front leg. Elevate your arms in a manner resembling the wings of a bird and maintain a level horizontal position while directing your gaze forward. Make an effort to maintain your equilibrium while envisioning yourself firmly rooted in this stance, establishing a deep connection with the ground as a formidable warrior.

To assume the bridge pose, assume a supine position. Exert pressure on the ground with your feet, elevating both your pelvis and thighs, thereby achieving an approximately 90-degree angle at your knees. Maintain equilibrium by distributing the weight of your body onto your shoulders and arms, which should remain aligned with your sides while grounded. Breathe in and out, ensuring that your shoulders and feet bear the weight, establishing a solid connection with the ground for both sections of your body as you progress through the series of yoga postures specifically crafted to unlock and energize your root chakra.

Yoga Asanas for Enhancing the Muladhara Chakra

To attain equilibrium in your root chakra, it is imperative to achieve a state of complete physical tranquility. Assume a relaxed and ergonomic posture, ideally with crossed legs and hands resting on the knees, grasping the Mundra associated with the Muladhara chakra. A Mundra is a manual gesture employed in the practice of yoga to accentuate and activate the energies residing within a specific cluster of energy along the spinal cord or chakra system. The mudra associated with the root chakra is formed by bringing the thumb and index finger together, creating the universally recognized gesture denoting "OK." Whilst maintaining this posture, direct your attention to the auditory perception of your breath as you inhale and exhale. Direct all your attention solely towards the auditory perception of your breathing, and you shall observe a gradual reduction in the incessant stream of thoughts within your mind, eventually leading to a state of thoughtlessness and mental liberation.

The ultimate objective of meditation is to achieve a state of complete absence of thoughts. The fundamental phonetic manifestation of the Muladhara chakra can be identified as 'lum.' Whilst assuming the previously indicated posture, emit auditory vibrations by expelling breath from the diaphragm and projecting it through the oral cavity. The fundamental phoneme is articulated as 'lung.' Sustain the phoneme while expelling a full exhalation, then repeat the process. During this process, endeavor to direct the energy residing within your physical form towards the vicinity of your pelvic region, while contemplating terrestrial elements such as the natural world, sustenance, progeny, and one's abode.

To concentrate the energy within a specific region of your body, envision the resonance generated by your vocal cords and direct it towards your pelvic region. Engage in this activity for approximately one minute on a daily basis, and you will commence experiencing a distinct sensation in your pelvic region as you engage in the practice of deliberate and gradual meditation. This indicates that you are effectively directing energy towards your Muladhara, prompting its progressive unblocking and facilitating the release of Kundalini energy throughout your physical being.

An alternative way to express the same idea in a formal tone would be: "The subsequent posture conducive to harmonizing the root chakra is the child pose." Whilst maintaining the seated position with crossed legs, bend forward and extend your arms as far as you can with your head directed towards the floor. Please ensure that your body is able to unwind and gently place your forehead on the surface below. Extend your arms forward and maintain contact between your hands and the floor. Envision yourself descending into the depths of the earth, merging harmoniously with the solid foundation beneath your feet. This will aid in the activation of the root chakra within your being.

The garland pose can be alternatively referred to as another posture. It necessitates assuming a posture where you maintain a squat position with your haunches lowered. Maintain a narrow and balanced stance by bringing your feet as close together as feasible, while simultaneously widening the distance between your thighs. Maintaining proper posture, exert pressure from your elbows against your inner thigh while joining your palms together. Once more, envision the gradual immersion of your feet into the soil, fostering the growth of roots that establish a deep connection and rootedness to the earth beneath you.

To initiate the standing forward bend, assume an upright stance. During the process of exhalation, lower your body forwards and endeavor to make contact between your hands and your toes. Exert downward pressure on the soles of your feet while reaching for each elbow with your hands. As you take a breath inward, elevate your upper body to a modest extent, then proceed to release the breath outward while gradually lowering it towards the surface. Reiterate these procedures for a few respiratory cycles. In this posture, permit the gravitational force to bear the entirety of your body weight, causing a gradual approach towards the earth's surface.

The mountain pose is exceedingly uncomplicated. Assume a stance where your feet are in close proximity, arms are positioned alongside your body, maintaining a straight posture with a firm back and flexed leg muscles. Maintain an upright and erect posture while envisioning your feet extending downwards, as if they are developing roots that deepen into the ground with each breath you take.

The next pose in the sequence is the warrior pose, which serves to facilitate the opening of your root chakra. For this specific role, execute a singular substantial movement by extending one of your legs forward and proceed to flex your anterior knee until it reaches a perfect right angle of 90 degrees. Ensure that your rear leg remains fully extended and engage your toes to apply pressure onto the ground, while firmly transferring your body weight onto your leading leg. Raise your arms in a manner that resembles the flapping wings of a bird, ensuring that they maintain a horizontal position while directing your gaze forward. Make an effort to maintain your equilibrium while mentally imagining yourself rooted and stable in this particular stance, establishing a strong connection with the earth as a warrior.

To assume the bridge pose, recline supine on the mat. With force exerted on the soles of your feet, elevate your pelvis and thighs upwards, resulting in the formation of an angle close to 90 degrees at your knee joints. Maintain equilibrium by distributing the weight of your body onto your shoulders and arms, ensuring they retain a positioned adjacency with the ground. Breathe deeply, allowing the breath to flow in and out of your body. Distribute the weight of your body on your shoulders and feet, establishing a stable connection with the ground. Engage in the series of yoga postures intended to unlock and stimulate your root chakra.

The Third Eye Chakra

The sixth chakra center, when its energy is properly aligned, is renowned for the extraordinary ability to perceive beyond ordinary visual limitations. Situated approximately in the region between the eyebrows, positioned just above the nose, one can find the sixth chakra center, commonly referred to as The Third Eye chakra. Although it is highly improbable that an additional ocular organ exists in the center of your cranium, the focal point of this particular chakra is dedicated to a different form of visual perception. This encompasses a spectrum of abilities ranging from enhanced clarity and perception to the ability to perceive alternate dimensions or realities. The Ajna chakra, also known as the Third Eye chakra, is associated with the essence of light and is characterized by the color violet. The profound level of lucidity associated with this chakra center transcends both temporal and spatial constraints. It possesses the capacity to facilitate introspection and discern one's inner truths, or to deeply perceive the external realm beyond the confines of mere visual perception.

In order to truly harness the Ajna, one must establish a profound connection to the heightened awareness of the Higher Self, even if it means tapping into only a fraction of its vast capabilities. This is a subjective interpretation based on my personal perspective. It is possible that alternative viewpoints may exist among others, and their differing perspectives are equally valid decisions they have made. Our perception of the world is limited by our individual levels of comprehension, which results in divergent interpretations of certain phenomena. Therefore, by harnessing this elevated level of perception, one can enhance their aptitude for comprehending the intricacies of the surrounding world. It affords you the opportunity to discern truth from falsity, in a manner of speaking. You adopt the position of an objective observer, enabling you to gain insights from various vantage points and enhance your comprehension of any given circumstance. There exists no discernible purpose or differentiation between righteousness and wickedness, solely the existence of what is. The Ajna facilitates the perception of both the broad and intricate aspects of a situation, enabling a comprehensive understanding of its complete extent, rather than limited knowledge based solely on a single instance.

The dissipation of the chakra's sense of greater clarity occurs due to an imbalance in this particular chakra. Individuals may experience cognitive haze and exhibit a propensity towards limited perspectives in their thinking. Experiencing a sense of confusion or feeling trapped, without any apparent solution, is an undesirable consequence arising from an imbalanced brow chakra. The frequency of your intuitive perceptions will decrease and their reliability will be diminished.

Furthermore, one can find themselves ensnared in contrived alternate realities, rendering them incapable of definitively discerning the authentic reality. Furthermore, certain individuals may also encounter a sense of disconnection from their spiritual counterparts, leading them to dismiss or negate anything existing beyond the boundaries of the tangible physical realm.

Restoring equilibrium to the brow chakra can be effortlessly achieved through the deliberate act of mindful breathing. Devoting one's attention solely to deeply inhaling and exhaling in a regulated manner can contribute to the restoration of equilibrium within the Ajna chakra as well as the overall system of chakras. Including natural foods that are violet or deep blue in color in your diet will also contribute to the wellness of your brow chakra. This encompasses fruit juices derived from deep-hued fruits such as blueberries, blackberries, eggplants, and similar varieties. Due to the fact that the Third Eye pertains to one's mental faculty of visualization, its activation occurs upon attempting to visualize objects or concepts independently of physical sight. It may appear unclear in the beginning, but with persistent experimentation, the process will become more streamlined and intricately defined. Your Ajna serves as the originator of dreams, hence it is advisable to maintain a dream journal to document them, progressively enhancing your ability to recollect dreams with heightened precision. This will undoubtedly provoke and fortify your brow chakra.

E.F.T (Emotional Freedom Technique)

The Emotional Freedom Technique, known as E.F.T or tapping, is a widely recognized method of healing that has been embraced universally. It has demonstrated remarkable efficacy in enhancing performance, regulating emotions, and promoting well-being across the dimensions of the chakra system. The Emotional Freedom Technique operates under the premise that persistent emotional concerns inevitably impede one's progress in various facets of life. It is commonly recognized that psychological stress can hinder the body's innate ability to heal itself. Emotional freedom technique is predicated upon the principle that the greater number of unresolved issues one successfully resolves, the higher the level of emotional liberation, tranquility, and happiness one can attain in their existence. EFT can effectively address chakra imbalances resulting from emotional disturbances, particularly past traumatic experiences, thereby fostering a state of optimal wellbeing and enhanced productivity.

Outlined herewith is a step-by-step guideline elucidating the procedure for implementing an Electronic Funds Transfer (EFT). You will require approximately half an hour in solitude.

1. Commence by seeking out a serene location, ideally outdoors on the grounds, where you can engage in EFT without any hindrances.

2. Please take a seat on a chair that provides comfort, ensuring that your feet rest flat on the floor in order to establish a grounding connection. It is also possible to recline, although it is preferable to focus on grounding, as it

allows for the transfer of source energy through the seven primary chakras into the earth.

3. In that particular posture, mentally envisage descending a luminous white beam, originating from the crown of your head (feel free to substitute the imagery of the white light with concepts such as affection, a divine resonance, radiant gold, or any visual representation that resonates more harmoniously with your personal preferences). Alternatively, one may choose to envision the illumination emanating from the soles of their feet.

4. As the illumination progressively diminishes within your cranium, please be attentive to any possible impediments that may arise. Should there be no impediments, you may proceed downward. Nevertheless, it is possible that you may encounter areas

of resistance, manifested as dark spots. Continue to visualize the radiant white light. Determine the underlying sentiment that is giving rise to the resistance, and make efforts to address and eliminate it.

5. Once the obstruction has been eliminated, ensure to examine for any additional obstructions within your crown chakra. If you come across any additional obstacles, make sure to address them accordingly.

6. While progressing through each chakra, one may come across impediments that cannot be fully resolved. That is okay. Imagined exerting force on the emotional impediment, shifting it aside, and allowing the pure, radiant light to freely pass through. The primary objective of the upcoming EFT session will be to address and resolve these remaining blockages.

7. One might observe correlations among the chakras while descending, and occasionally find it necessary to retrace their steps in order to resolve certain associations.

8. Verify whether all the chakras have been freed from emotional obstructions by allowing the unimpeded passage of pure white light through, proceeding systematically from the base to the crown, encompassing the seven chakras. It is advised that you rise to your feet for this segment.

9. Once the entire set of obstacles has been eliminated from your chakras, employ the law of attraction and engage in a systematic visualization of the desired transformation. In the absence of any emotional barriers that were addressed during the session, you should experience a heightened sense of its intensity. Please ensure that you are

conscious of it by securely establishing it. Engaging in this particular context may potentially activate further emotional barriers; it is advisable to address and resolve them accordingly.

10. Once you have identified the vibration of your desire, you can opt to embrace that sentiment throughout the duration of your day. The greater the frequency at which the internal vibrations align with your aspirations, the more expeditiously they will materialize.

Heart Chakra:

Positioned: centrally within the thoracic region

Following the transmission of energy from the crown chakra to the third eye and the throat chakra, it ultimately descends to reside within the heart chakra. This constitutes the fundamental cause and origin of cardiovascular diseases. If you frequently experience feelings of envy and profound sorrow towards others, this subject matter will unquestionably resonate with you. The heart chakra entails the capacity to experience and reciprocate love in an unhindered manner.

Indications of an imbalanced heart chakra:
- Enviousness paired with a reluctance to witness others' success - Feelings of

envy intertwined with a lack of desire to witness the accomplishments of others - A sense of jealousy coupled with an aversion towards witnessing others' achievements

- Holding deep animosity towards others and oneself, frequently fixating on unfavorable aspects

- the individual undertaking the rescue operation or the person facing oppression

- Experiencing an emotional transition or having undergone a prolonged period that continues to influence you

- Being stressful

Balancing method:

- Psychotherapy can be valuable as it facilitates the expression of emotions, which is essential for the healing of the heart chakra.

- Maintaining a personal diary and documenting one's emotions, thereby expressing any negative sentiments.

- Engaging in self-reflection and prioritizing the cultivation of positive emotions while actively working to purge negative emotions from within oneself

Solar Plexus:

Located: Upper abdomen

Have you ever observed individuals with limited aspirations, profound shyness, consistently maintaining a lowered gaze, and someone who has never assumed leadership roles in any capacity? Indeed, if that is the case, these manifestations can be attributed to the solar plexus chakra. The Solar Plexus chakra serves as the foundation for our ego, identity, personality, and the essence of our being emanates from this center. The crux of the matter lies in individual empowerment.

Indications of an immoderate abundance of solar plexus chakra energy:
- Experiencing heightened stress levels and exhaustion.
- Experiencing an intense emotional outburst.

Indications of depleted energy in the solar plexus chakra:
- Experiencing a sense of life's circumstances working against you
- Not being active

Balancing method:
- Standing for yourself
- Exercising cognitive control over your thoughts, strategically determining the approaches to navigate and conclude various situations.
- Having your voice acknowledged - Exercising your right to be heard - Making a meaningful contribution to the conversation - Asserting your viewpoint

and ensuring it is taken into account - Expressing your opinions and having them recognized - Making a valuable input to the discussion - Advocating for your perspectives and opinions - Raising your voice and ensuring it is heard
- Lowering your ego

"Signs denoting a harmonized solar plexus chakra:
- Displaying a proactive attitude and a readiness to assume a leadership role
- Possessing self-assurance and a clear sense of identity and future direction
- Motivated to fulfill responsibilities and commitments
- Engaged and actively progressing - Proactive and achieving tasks - Enthusiastic and accomplishing objectives - Productive and engaged in tasks - Diligent and effectively completing tasks
Sacral Chakra

Situated: Extending from the lower abdomen to the pelvic region

The Sacral chakra can be regarded as the focal point within the body, acting as an energetic vortex that governs one's capacity for creativity, as well as the degree of pleasure and satisfaction one derives from their activities and experiences.

Indications of an obstructed sacral chakra:
- No creativity
- Lack of ideas
- Incapable of deriving happiness from existence - Struggling to discover contentment in the journey of life - Facing a profound inability to experience joy in living

Balancing method:

There is no definitive method to achieve equilibrium in this particular chakra in isolation. If this energy center is imbalanced and inactive, it implies that all other chakras are also imbalanced and obstructed. This particular energy center is influenced by the activation and openness of all other chakras, and once they are activated and unblocked, this chakra will naturally open as well. If one's Sacral chakra is obstructed, it is likely that one's other chakras are also blocked, possibly even all of the chakras.

Balanced Sacral Chakra indicators:
- You consistently generate innovative and imaginative ideas.
- One derives pleasure and discerns it in the mundane aspects of life.

Root Chakra

Situated at the lowermost point of the vertebral column.

It is no mere happenstance that the root chakra is positioned at the lowermost point of the spine, as it represents an intricately interconnected energy center that serves as the foundation for all your actions and endeavors. When contemplating the term 'base', it evokes thoughts of the underpinning, which signifies the fundamental origin and catalyst thereof. Your prevalent sense of insecurity, accompanied by feelings of being unanchored and lacking a sense of safety, can be attributed to an inherent imbalance in your root chakra.

Indications of a blocked root chakra:
- Experiencing a lack of security and lacking a support system
- Unmoored and lacking foundations
- Disconnected and lacking a solid base
- Untethered and lacking rootedness
- Adrift and lacking a sense of grounding -

Unanchored and devoid of a solid foundation.
- Lacking a firm footing - Absence of a strong groundwork - Insufficient basis

Balancing method:
- Engaging in meditative practices and acknowledging the inherent connection to a divine entity known as God.
- I beseech the divine entity to grant you the ability to perceive and acknowledge his intervention in your life, leading to a strengthened conviction in his unwavering support for you.
- Gaining a thorough understanding of one's fundamental principles and exploring their origins, subsequently endeavoring to transform and establish them upon a stable and fresh groundwork.

Balanced root chakra indicators:

- Experiencing a sense of security and personal safety - Emotionally and physically protected - Being confident in one's safety and well-being - Enjoying a state of being secure and free from harm.

- Having the assurance that someone will provide support and assistance - Understanding that there is someone who will look out for you and offer help if needed - Being confident in the knowledge that someone is there to provide backup and assistance in difficult situations - Having the peace of mind knowing that someone is standing by to offer support and assistance

- You are able to attract financial resources effortlessly as a result of your positive vibrations.

The Sacral Chakra

The sacral chakra is symbolized by the hue of orange. The sacral chakra is associated with matters pertaining to both sensuality and emotions. Many contemporary coaches assert that it symbolizes the earthly cravings of individuals, but this Chakra embodies a more encompassing perception of emotions and communication. If this chakra is unblocked, you will experience a sense of freedom and liberation. Your emotional capacity will remain unrestricted, and you may experience a plethora of emotions without exhibiting excessive emotional behavior.

In a moderate measure, upon the activation of this chakra, you will experience enhanced sociability and embrace a light-hearted nature, while encountering no hindrances in your intimate relationships. Nevertheless, should this sacral chakra be sealed or marginally unsealed, it is anticipated to induce emotional frigidity and seclusion. One may observe a tendency towards self-centeredness and a lack of confidence in social interactions.

Conversely, should this specific chakra showcase heightened activity, perpetual emotional states may ensue. The merest hint of a stirring instant will elicit an exceptional emotional reaction from you. Typical issues can induce feelings of stress and sadness. Individuals have been observed to exhibit heightened sexual urges while experiencing a concurrently dissatisfied state when this chakra is excessively activated.

There exist several practices aimed at optimizing the effectiveness of this chakra. Given that this chakra is renowned for its inclination to lack control and prove challenging to harness, the utmost significance lies in the cultivation of stillness and unwavering mental concentration during the corresponding exercises. A widely favored practice for accessing and harmonizing this particular Chakra is elucidated in the subsequent passage.

Assume a kneeling position, ensuring your back is upright yet at ease. Place your hands in your lap, ensuring that your palms are facing upwards. Place your left hand beneath your right hand, ensuring that the palm of your left hand makes contact with the dorsal side of your right hand's fingers.

Ensure that both thumbs make contact with one another in a delicate manner. Upon assuming this posture, allow yourself to unwind and direct your focus towards comprehending and pursuing the significance and purpose of the sacral chakra. After achieving a state of tranquility, proceed to recite the mantra "VAM" and, concurrently, concentrate on the essence of the sacral chakra, while striving to rid your mind of any extraneous thoughts. It is recommended to maintain your stance and persist with the "VAM" chant until you experience a state of complete relaxation and emotional well-being.

Initially, it may require a significant amount of time to attain this state of mind. However, as you progress and acquire greater mastery over the barriers encountered during meditation, the attainment of this objective will gradually become more effortless. At this juncture, it becomes necessary to incorporate more advanced exercises in order to facilitate the continued progression of the sacral chakra.

The Throat Chakra

Throat Chakra Basics

T

The fifth chakra, known as the Throat chakra, is positioned at the midpoint of the neck. Concerned with the facets of communication and self-expression, this chakra assists us in nurturing our capacity to assert ourselves and articulate our authentic voice. The Throat chakra is referred to as Vishuddha in Sanskrit, denoting its significance as a source of purification. By expressing our thoughts and beliefs with integrity and confidence, we allow our true selves to manifest in an unadulterated and genuine manner. The bodily regions that are interconnected with this particular chakra encompass the thyroid gland, the region of the throat, the neck, the jaw, the mouth, and the vocal apparatus. The color blue symbolizes the fifth chakra, while its bija mantra is Ham, which can be pronounced as "hŏm."

A Healthy Throat Chakra

When our Throat chakra is balanced and functioning optimally, we possess the capacity to articulate our thoughts and emotions with clarity, authenticity, and diplomacy. When in a state of equilibrium, this chakra grants us assurance in the articulation of our thoughts. In addition, we have the capacity to actively engage in attentive listening and create a supportive environment where individuals can openly articulate their thoughts.

Throat Chakra Imbalances

An obstructed Throat chakra can result in manifestations such as social reticence, apprehension towards vocalizing opinions, or difficulties in expressing oneself verbally. In the event of an excessive activation of this particular chakra, it is probable that an inclination towards a dominant mode of speech and an imbalance between speaking and attentive listening may manifest. Our language has the potential to turn vulgar or even offensive. Physical manifestations that may arise due to an imbalance in the Throat chakra encompass symptoms such as coughing, allergic reactions, and conditions affecting the throat and ears.

Crystals & Stones

Gemstones in various hues of blue possess the ability to effectively harmonize the energy within the Throat chakra. Blue lace agate, sodalite, and angelite are merely a handful of exemplifications. In the event that one chooses to incorporate stones into their meditation practice, it is advised to exercise caution and refrain from utilizing stones of considerable size or weight. If any form of discomfort should arise directly in the throat area, it is recommended to consider alternative approaches such as placing stones on either side of the neck or simply holding them.

Foods & Herbs

Blueberries are a discernible selection for promoting the nourishment of the Throat chakra, however, other fruits are also advised for this purpose. These fruits encompass sour varieties such as lemons and grapefruit, alongside sweet varieties like apples, plums, and peaches. Furthermore, it is advisable to consume beverages that possess soothing or hydrating properties for the throat, such as herbal tea or coconut water. A few herbal options worth considering would be chamomile, licorice root, and elderberry.

Essential Oils

Frankincense is a valuable essential oil that is renowned for its correlation with eloquent communication. Lemongrass and eucalyptus are alternative recommendations that would be beneficial to incorporate into your practice of healing the Throat chakra.

Chakras and Their Interaction with the Physical Body

Throughout the ages, the sages of various civilizations have conveyed the notion that our physical beings emanate an electromagnetic field, serving as the wellspring of the cosmic vitalizing energy. Every one of the primary organs within the body possesses its own distinctive electromagnetic field, and when these fields converge, they form the intricate and multi-layered auras that define our being. The occurrence of perturbations in the vibrational frequencies within our auras gives rise to the manifestation of bodily ailments. According to a study conducted by Dr. Valerie Hunt in 1977, it was demonstrated that the manipulation of aura energy can effectively restore equilibrium to the chakras and facilitate the healing of various ailments.

A seasoned practitioner possesses the capability to perform a manual examination of a patient's body, whereby they can discern subtle disruptions or incongruities within the various strata of the aura. Fluctuations in temperature or variations in the rate of energy flow serve as indicators of disparities within the chakras. The patient relinquishes all preconceived notions and anticipations and assumes a receptive role as a conduit, enabling the healer to channel energy with precision and tailor it to cater to the patient's requirements.

When an individual establishes a secure connection with the earth, the conveyance of energy ensues, ascending through the feet and legs to ultimately reach the Base Chakra. This vital energy is then employed to attain equilibrium in the functioning of the reproductive glands, such as the gonads, ovaries, and testes, thereby facilitating the regulation of menstrual cycles, estrogen and progesterone release in women, and testosterone release in men. The fundamental chakra subsequently transmits the terrestrial energy along the spinal column towards the upper chakras. The functionality of our Base Chakra pertains to our fundamental necessities. Consequently, when this chakra is imbalanced or severed from its connection with the earth, we manifest an excessive preoccupation with alimentation and sexual desires. Additionally, the Base Chakra promotes the instinctual drive for reproduction and the formation of familial units.

When the Base Chakra detects peril or tension, it signals the Sacral Chakra, prompting an activation of the adrenal glands in a fight or flight response. The Sacral Chakra reacts by initiating the secretion of adrenaline, thereby inducing hormonal alterations within the body. This chakra is also responsible for the regulation of cortisol release, which impacts the body's capacity to metabolize carbohydrates, protein, and aldosterone, a hormone that enables the kidneys to retain sodium and water. The Sacral Chakra also influences the urinary system, the kidneys, and the way our bodies process fluids. Physical ailments such as colitis, lumbar discomfort, irritable bowel syndrome, impaired nutrient absorption, and bladder malignancies can all be attributed to an imbalanced state of the Sacral Chakra.

Situated amidst the region delineated by the navel and lower segment of the sternum, the Solar Plexus Chakra exhibits an affiliation with bodily areas characterized by heightened reactivity towards stressful stimuli. Blocked or unbalanced Solar Plexus Chakra has been found to correlate with digestive concerns, cancer, and diabetes. The vitality of the Solar Plexus Chakra exerts an impact on the functioning of the pancreas, initiating either the secretion of insulin to decrease elevated blood sugar levels or the generation of glucagons to elevate low blood sugar levels. Headaches, neck aches, respiratory difficulties, hypertension, and gastrointestinal issues are all interconnected with stress, and all of these ailments can be alleviated through the restoration of equilibrium in the Solar Plexus Chakra.

Located at the midpoint of the thorax, the cardiac chakra exercises influence over both the organ of the heart and the intricate network of blood vessels that comprises the circulatory system. The circulatory system facilitates the transportation of nutrients, water, and oxygen to various parts of the body, while effectively eliminating waste products through the pulmonary and hepatic organs, in addition to bolstering the function of the immune system. If the equilibrium of our Heart Chakra is disrupted due to physical trauma or emotional distress, it has the potential to interfere with the regular rhythm of our heart and contribute to the onset of ailments and infections affecting the cardiac muscles and valves. The Heart Chakra is also interconnected with the thymus gland, which triggers the body's defensive mechanisms in reaction to sickness and physical trauma.

The Throat Chakra exerts an influence on various bodily components including the auditory system, pharynx, nasal passages, and the respiratory system. Additionally, it has an impact on the thyroid gland, situated in the cervical region, which governs the equilibrium of calcium and phosphate concentrations, cellular restoration, as well as the pace of cerebral and bodily development. A wide range of ailments, encompassing conditions such as sore throat, fatigue, hyperthyroidism, as well as digestive and weight issues, can be effectively addressed through the process of restoring balance and vitality to the Throat Chakra. Respiratory difficulties are likewise linked to the Throat Chakra and can be alleviated through the practice of specialized breathing techniques.

Situated amidst the brow ridge, in close proximity to the nasal bridge, the Third Eye exerts its influence upon the cranium, ocular organs, and auditory structures. It is additionally associated with the pituitary and pineal glands. The endocrine glands generally function cohesively under the guidance of the pituitary gland. In the event of their malfunction, their operation is characterized by the excessive or inadequate release of hormones. The pineal gland assumes the responsibility of regulating sleep, mood, sexuality, and menstrual cycles through the secretion of melanin and seratonin. Should these elements be in a state of imbalance, it will consequently lead to an imbalance in the functioning of the Third Eye.

The Crown Chakra is believed to be situated either at the crown of the head or slightly above it, near the area where the anterior fontanelle is present on an infant's skull. It has been suggested that the closure of the fontanelle area in infants corresponds with the sealing of a child's heightened awareness of the boundless and everlasting universe. In the majority of individuals, these aspects are promptly overshadowed by the intricacies of one's personality, ego, and physical form, only to resurface when contemplations on mortality arise. This detachment from the boundless expanse impacts all of our physiological systems and processes. The Crown Chakra exerts its influence on the pineal and pituitary glands, and any disruption in its equilibrium can lead to conditions such as headaches, epilepsy, hypertension, paralysis, and Parkinson's disease.

The chakras exert an influence on the entirety of our physical body and its systems, much akin to the control exerted by our major organs. The chakras operate collectively, under the guidance of the Crown Chakra, to facilitate the flow of energy throughout the body and maintain hormonal balance. The presence of imbalances within our chakras leads to corresponding imbalances in our overall state of well-being. Their upkeep is indispensable for our physical functioning and the maximization of our life's pleasures.

Indications and Manifestations of Disruption in the Cardiac Chakra

There are various circumstances that occur throughout one's life, including experiences such as bereavement following the loss of a beloved individual, instances of separation, divorce, emotional mistreatment, forsakenness, infidelity, among others. that can potentially inflict significant harm. Each of these factors will lead to the impairment and disruption of your Heart Chakra. If you are in search of your injured child, it will become apparent that they are situated within your Heart Chakra.

Potential physical manifestations one may encounter encompass arm discomfort, cardiovascular afflictions, respiratory ailments such as asthma and lung disease, complications within the lymphatic system, as well as issues pertaining to the upper back and shoulders.

Emotional disturbances encompass various matters concerning your injured heart, such as feelings of desertion, resentment, envy, animosity, an overwhelming attachment to others, and a dread of solitude.

The experience of emotional distress can lead to the manifestation of physical maladies. Prior to attaining success, it is imperative that you address and overcome your emotional wounds. The initial step you must undertake is to acquire the ability to cultivate self-love. Engaging in this remarkably potent preliminary action can greatly aid you in attaining fortification of your Heart Chakra.

An imbalanced Heart Chakra can manifest in various indicators, such as exhibiting excessive control, engaging in defensive behavior, experiencing reluctance to release attachments, displaying a tendency towards criticism or skepticism, adopting a more reserved demeanor, or demonstrating possessive tendencies.

How to Attain Equilibrium in Your Heart Chakra

Having achieved equilibrium in the Heart Chakra, individuals will possess a remarkable capacity for embracing others, finding contentment in the present moment despite its flaws, and cultivating self-compassion. You shall henceforth be relieved from occupying your time in an unfavorable milieu. Life will appear abundant and you will experience a profound sense of self-assuredness, enabling you to surmount any obstacle with ease.

It is Essential to Embrace Environmental Sustainability

It is recommended to venture into nature at this time and immerse oneself in the diverse shades of green present in the surroundings. They intend to initiate the recuperation phase. Commence engaging in leisurely strolls or embarking on nature excursions outside the urban environment. Allocate a period of time in the vicinity of a lake. Seek out green space. If leaving the city is not feasible, it is highly likely that one could locate green areas such as parks within almost every city or town. It is advisable to explore and identify one such area. It constitutes a critical aspect in the process of emotional recovery.

Furthermore, it is imperative to incorporate green into various aspects of your life, such as maintaining a balanced diet with green foods, adorning green attire, and incorporating green hues into your surroundings through artistic means, should you find it aesthetically pleasing.

Visualize and Breathe Green

It is not solely important to adopt an environmentally friendly lifestyle, but it is imperative that you also start conceptualizing and embodying a sustainable mindset. Take a deep breath and mentally envision a robust, lucid green light entering your heart center, positioned in the midst of your sternum and slightly beneath your shoulder blades. Allow this gentle green light to permeate your entire being, saturating every inch of your body. As you engage in the act of exhaling, sense the departure of any lingering negative energy from your physical being. Exercise caution when exhaling and direct your attention towards the constructive energy derived from inhalation rather than the detrimental energy of exhalation.

Embrace the qualities of love and extend your love to others.

Please permit yourself to receive love and ensure that you prioritize self-love. Frequently, the concept of 'us' eludes our consciousness. It is imperative to cultivate a love for fellow individuals that is devoid of conditions or self-interest. This method offers a remarkable opportunity for you to purify and harmonize your Heart Chakra.

Do avoid being a perpetually pessimistic individual.

You are familiar with the individual designated as the Naysayer, who consistently exhibits a pessimistic outlook regarding their current circumstances and exhibits a perpetual inclination to seek an improved situation elsewhere. One might find it unforeseen to realize that the grass is not, in fact, greener on the alternative side. It is inherent in human behavior to assume the role of a pessimistic individual or a harbinger of negativity. Endeavor to refrain from adopting a pessimistic outlook on your surroundings and from incessantly criticizing everything in your vicinity. It is essential to express gratitude for one's blessings.

It's Yoga Time

It is evident that you have likely observed a consistent underlying connection among all of your chakras, which pertains to the practice of yoga. In instances where there is a blockage in the Heart Chakra, it is often observed that the corresponding blockage in the Throat Chakra also occurs.

The camel pose is highly beneficial in promoting equilibrium within the body. Direct your attention towards the stretch and ensure that you maintain a receptive posture. Online, one can access more comprehensive information regarding yoga asanas.

Time has come for us to extend our forgiveness

Clinging to feelings of anger, regret, hurt, and grief from the past hinders one's progress and invariably results in an obstruction of the Heart Chakra. It is advisable to demonstrate promptness in extending forgiveness and allowing the past to remain in the past.

The act of forgiveness does not revolve around the individual being forgiven; rather, it primarily concerns oneself. They exhibit indifference towards the matter, yet by doing so, you empower yourself with tranquility and enable personal progress. This may pose a considerable difficulty and challenge, necessitating the assistance of a professional. Exercise patience, wholeheartedly embrace your current endeavors, and cultivate self-love and contentment in your present circumstances.

This particular chakra can be found situated within the upper abdominal region, in close proximity to the stomach.

What is the realm that is under the influence of the Solar Plexus Chakra?

This particular chakra governs the aspects of ego, self-assurance, and cognition. It synergizes with the Sacral chakra by addressing one's cognitive state, albeit without engaging with the emotional aspect in this particular context.

The color yellow exerts an impact on the solar plexus (a mnemonic for this can be derived from the association of the term "solar" or "sun" with the color yellow.)

Indications of an Obstruction in the Solar Plexus

As this chakra governs cognition and the faculties of thought, it exercises control over one's ego, fostering a persistent drive for achievement and lifelong pursuit of knowledge. An obstruction in this region can severely impair your overall state of well-being.

In the event of an inequilibrium in the energy of your solar plexus, one may experience a perceived inadequacy in self-assurance. Your sense of humor may also be impacted, as you might experience a diminished capacity to appreciate wit and begin to perceive matters with excessive gravity.

Consequently, there exists a close correlation between the energies of the sacral and solar plexus, whereby a decline in confidence poses challenges in effectively recognizing and embracing emotions in a manner that promotes well-being and progress.

This chakra serves as the wellspring of one's self-restraint and self-regulation, playing a pivotal role in fostering a harmonious and salubrious existence.

Individuals who possess a deficiency in self-discipline are inherently more susceptible to succumbing to addiction and substance abuse, as well as finding themselves in unfavorable life circumstances as a result of poor decision-making.

Additionally, their lives may experience a state of stagnation as a result of their lack of determination to persevere through challenging circumstances in order to achieve their desired goals.

What is the Impact of a Solar Plexus Blockage on Your Overall Wellness?

Both your physical and mental well-being can be compromised in this scenario, and failing to address the issue could potentially lead to hazards. One potential issue of mild significance that may occur is a deficiency in memory.

Disruptions in the equilibrium of the Solar Plexus have an impact on the cognitive processing of information, leading to a scenario where your brain may perceive information that was once deemed significant as relatively dispensable. This can pose challenges in acquiring novel abilities or knowledge.

A state of uneasiness and distress may ensue if there is an imbalance in the energy of your solar plexus. Failure to address this matter could potentially manifest as a significant impediment to attaining the desired quality of life.

Agoraphobia exemplifies an instance of anxiety that has become unmanageable; when it reaches this level, there are no instant solutions available. Anxiety can also create significant tension in your interpersonal relationships, impeding your ability to let down your guard and establish genuine connections with others.

Digestion may also suffer. The Solar Plexus chakra has historically been associated with the proper functioning of the digestive system, and revitalizing this chakra can prove to be a beneficial approach in addressing issues within this domain.

What are the various stages of the chakra system?

The various stages of the chakra system are perpetually determined by the energy present within the chakras. Before delving into the various techniques employed for chakra healing and balance, it is imperative to familiarize oneself with the four crucial stages that underpin this process and contribute to overall well-being.

Active Phase

The name of the phase explicitly conveys the intended meaning of the phase. This is an ideal state for your chakra to be in. At this juncture, your chakra is operating flawlessly. As an illustrative example, let us examine the root chakra. It has been communicated to you that this particular chakra consistently aids in comprehending one's condition during a fight or flight circumstance. When this operates effectively, you will consistently be able to ensure that you maintain optimal physical and mental well-being. The luminosity of your Aura will consistently be enhanced when all the chakras are harmoniously aligned in this state.

Underactive Phase

This stage is akin to the student who consistently maintains a quiet demeanor during classroom discussions. He simply requires a catalyst to enhance his performance in the classroom. This chakra also requires a gentle nudge in order to activate its functionality. When faced with a challenging circumstance, one will observe that the functionality of this particular chakra has become optimized. Regardless of whether the changes occur in the environment or within your own body, you will still have the capability to elicit a bodily response in order to ensure your own protection.

Passive Phase

This is the stage in which your body experiences serenity and relaxation. This occurs when your chakra enters a state of restfulness, signifying that the energy within your body has achieved equilibrium. This pertains to the perpetual equilibrium between the energy within and surrounding one's corporeal being. This task is equivalent to the process of equilibrating a chemical equation in the context of a Chemistry examination.

Overactive Phase

This phenomenon occurs when one experiences intense emotional states. You will discover that the subtle energy residing within the chakras demonstrates remarkable susceptibility to the various occurrences transpiring in the surrounding environment. These chakras may potentially possess a substantial amount of energy, resulting in a state of imbalance that manifests in both physical and mental aspects.

Why is it important that you balance your chakras?

Each individual chakra within your physical being possesses a distinct function that holds significance, facilitating the overarching goal of maintaining a state of both mental and physical well-being. In the preceding , it was elucidated that the chakras are interconnected with various anatomical regions and serve to harmonize the energies inherent to each specific bodily locale. It is postulated that these energies serve as the underlying cause of your existence. The chakras operate to generate an energetic field known as an aura, by channeling the energy in a manner that aligns with the body's acceptance. When an individual achieves balance in one chakra, they will be capable of harmonizing all remaining chakras. This occurrence is attributed to the alignment of the chakras with one another.

The auras emanating from your chakras serve as communication signals to both your surroundings and yourself. The communications consist of electromagnetic impulses, which are subject to various factors, with emotions having the most profound influence on them. Through the emanation of your auras, the chakras establish connections with both the surrounding environment and the various dimensions. Your auras significantly influence your responses to the world and interpersonal interactions. When you encountered new individuals, you might have experienced either a favorable or unfavorable impression. This phenomenon arises as a result of the compelling interplay among the distinct energies encapsulated within your aura.

While perusing this literary work, one will undoubtedly discern the transformative alterations that shall ensue within the intricate network of one's chakras, thereby impacting the vibrational energy housed within said chakras. You will observe that specific alterations are exclusively implemented when one is in a state of poor health or illness. Furthermore, this book will provide you with insights into various possible alterations you can implement, enabling you to effectively harmonize the energy flow within the chakras. One will have the capacity to discern the imbalance of their chakras and subsequently effectuate the necessary adjustments. In the forthcoming s, you will be presented with a comprehensive array of techniques that can be utilized with optimal efficacy to restore equilibrium to the chakras.

Swadhisthana, the Sacral

On a daily basis, we come across individuals who vary in their resemblances to us, ranging from those who are strikingly similar to those who hold stark differences. Although the majority of people we come across will remain unfamiliar, a select few interactions have the potential to develop into meaningful friendships. As evidenced by the previously mentioned exercise, it is apparent that our lives are filled with numerous individuals whom we are acquainted with, hold affection for, value, and deeply respect.

The Swadhisthana, also known as the Sacral Chakra, can be found in the region spanning from the base of the spine to the navel, approximately at a distance of 2 inches. In relation to the other six Chakras, this particular Chakra energy node within our body is situated as the second most inferior, positioned only inches beyond the Root Chakra.

The Sacral represents a diverse range of sentiments and characteristics, although its predominant association lies in our capacity to establish relationships with and embrace others. Thus, it is rational to perceive the Sacral as the energetic nexus of our physical being, from which spring forth our sentiments, emotions, sensuality, intimacy, and sensations of gratification. Due to its intrinsic association with these potent sentiments centered around affection and desire, the Sacral chakra assumes a pivotal role in fostering and sustaining all our interpersonal bonds, irrespective of the intensity of amorous sentiment imbued within them. To put it differently, the Sacral occupies a comparable position in our profound connections with enduring friends just as it does in our intimate and romantic involvements.

Opening Your Sacral

Particularly in contemporary society, where one's success is closely tied to the capacity to conceal emotions, exhibit self-restraint, and regulate cognitive processes, the Sacral Chakra encounters challenges in sustaining equilibrium amidst the remaining six Chakras. If you find yourself encountering an imbalance or a closed Sacral, there is no need for excessive concern. Similar to the core, certain dietary choices and physical activities can be employed to address an asymmetrical or restricted Sacral.

Indications of an Enclosed Sacral

Similar to what was previously discussed in 1, numerous additional symptoms manifest when individuals encounter imbalances in their Chakra system. Nevertheless (and I will proceed to do so with the subsequent 5 Chakras), I have incorporated the most prevalent and readily observable indications of an unbalanced or obstructed Sacral.

Decreased libido

Hormonal imbalance

Irritability

Lower back pain

Sexual obsession or aggression

Root-Opening Foods

Assorted varieties of nuts including peanuts, walnuts, pistachios, almonds, and more.

Citrus fruits such as oranges and tangerines, as well as other food items with an orange hue.

Varieties of melons include watermelon, honeydew melon, and cantaloupe.

Strawberries

Passion fruit

Root-Opening Exercises

Cobra pose: As Chakras exhibit a strong correlation with meditation, numerous Chakra-activating practices presented within this book originate from mindful exercises. The cobra pose is no exclusion. To successfully conclude this exercise, it is advisable to locate a level and resilient surface (For instance, the floor would be more desirable in comparison to utilizing your bed).

1. Assume a prone position on the floor, facing downwards. Ensure that you maintain firm contact between your thighs, along with the bony structure of your pelvic area, and the surface of the ground.

2. Ensure that your hands are positioned directly beneath your shoulders and proceed to draw your elbows inward, towards your torso.

3. While you breathe in, proceed to lengthen your arms and elevate your chest from the surface, ensuring that your thighs and pelvic bone remain firmly grounded.

4. Assuming a vertical posture, retract your shoulders and maintain this stance

for a duration of 2 minutes. Slowly inhale and exhale.

5. After the lapse of 2 minutes, gradually descend to the initial position, expelling air from your lungs at a deliberate pace.

Pelvic Thrusts: Given the close connection between the Sacral region and elements such as intimacy, sexuality, and pleasure, it is logical to propose that engaging in a physically expressive movement, often linked to sexual undertones, can be regarded as a physical exercise aimed at reestablishing equilibrium and promoting the reopening of a dormant or unbalanced Sacral. To successfully carry out this activity, assume a stable standing position with your feet firmly planted on the ground, maintaining a distance equivalent to the width of your shoulders. While maintaining a relaxed stance with your arms by your sides, gradually move your pelvis in a forward direction while taking a breath in, and then in a backward direction while exhaling. Do this 20 times.

Methods to Unblock a Congested Throat Chakra

Restoring balance to an obstructed throat chakra necessitates more than merely relying on a throat lozenge. However, there exist distinctive approaches through which one can genuinely effect positive change.

"Engage in physical activities such as:

Compose Personal Correspondence to Yourself

This is another example of an exercise that may appear frivolous, yet possesses genuine benefits. Engaging in the act of letter writing to oneself may prove beneficial in the process of alleviating and relinquishing emotional burdens that have persisted over a significant period. It possesses a remarkable therapeutic quality, enabling individuals to access their innermost being and effectively resolve deep-rooted issues. In instances where articulating one's emotions becomes challenging, composing personal letters can serve as a highly effective means to initiate open communication.

Engage in Inner Child Communication

Each individual possesses an internal youthful essence that necessitates proper care and nurturing. Furthermore, building upon the aforementioned practice of composing letters to oneself, it is advisable to endeavor to engage in conversation with one's inner child. Engaging in a cognitive exercise of conceptual nature, it is possible to mitigate a significant portion of an obstructed throat chakra through the utilization of compassionate communication with your inner child.

Neck exercises pertaining to yoga

There exist several highly effective yoga exercises for the neck that can be utilized to alleviate obstruction of the throat chakra. One of these movements, known as the "neck release technique," entails maintaining an upright posture and gently swiveling the neck from right to left while inhaling deeply and exhaling slowly. After engaging in this activity for a brief duration, proceed to incline your head in the direction of your left shoulder, subsequently positioning your left hand on the opposing side of your cranium. Subsequently, duplicate this procedure with your contralateral shoulder. Initially, one may experience a slight discomfort in mastering the movement, however, with practice, one will familiarize oneself and observe significant enhancement in the function of their throat chakra.

Engage in contemplation without speaking

Occasionally, a brief period of silence proves to be the most appropriate remedy, and when it concerns the throat chakra, this sentiment holds particularly true. Through engaging in a silent meditation practice, individuals have the opportunity to deliberately decelerate their mental activity, enabling them to attentively discern the true messages originating from their chakra. In doing so, they create an environment wherein the obstacles impeding the optimal functioning of their throat chakra dissolve and dissipate. Discover a serene and tranquil location in which to engage in the practice of meditation, and you shall experience a notable improvement in your well-being.

Breathing Exercises

To restore the functionality of your obstructed throat chakra, one may participate in invigorating breathing techniques that facilitate the removal of the blockage. In order to achieve this, locate a serene environment devoid of any distractions and assume a kneeling position on a cushion or plush floor covering. Assume a kneeling position and secure your hands behind your back, grasping your ankles. While maintaining this posture, retract your head and initiate a series of profound inhalations. Perform this action for a brief duration, and subsequently loosen your grasp on your ankles, allowing yourself to descend forward until the crown of your head comes into contact with the floor. Maintain this posture momentarily, then inhale deeply and return to the initial position in order to commence the breathing exercise anew. Engage in the repetition of this particular exercise several times, or as frequently as you deem appropriate.

Once you undertake the aforementioned action, you will promptly begin to perceive a tangible disparity in your emotional state.

Practice Forgiveness

The act of granting forgiveness exerts a tangible influence on our throat chakra, as by extending forgiveness to others, we can alleviate a considerable weight from this energy center. Bitterness can manifest as a detrimental obstruction to the proper functioning of your throat chakra. As previously indicated in preceding s of this literary work, it is imperative to diligently cultivate the virtue of forgiveness to the greatest extent possible. It does not entail that you must disregard the grievous harm that has been inflicted upon you. In the event that you have experienced a carjacking and have been held at gunpoint, it is not anticipated that you can effortlessly erase that traumatic experience from your recollection; however, it is imperative that you make a genuine effort to progress and cope with the situation to the best of your ability. It can be challenging at times, but it is essential to conscientiously endeavor to let go of past issues and actively engage in forgiveness in the present.

Express your thoughts

As previously stated in the preceding section, refraining from expressing your views when you feel an inclination to do so can result in an obstruction of your throat chakra. Choosing to remain silent ultimately results in feelings of remorse and the internalization of emotions. Therefore, to circumvent this issue, it is imperative that you express your thoughts candidly when the opportunity presents itself.

Throat Chakra Stones

Similar to numerous other chakras, empirical evidence supports the notion that the utilization of throat chakra stones can facilitate the unblocking of the healing channels associated with this particular chakra. These stones facilitate the activation of vibrational pathways that effectively alleviate blockages within the chakras, restoring their optimal functioning.

Recite Affirmations Regularly

Once more, in similar fashion to numerous other obstructed chakras, the mere repetition of a handful of affirming mantras can have remarkable effects in reestablishing the flux of energy. Reiterate affirmations to oneself, such as "I possess the freedom to express myself" and "I have the capacity to vocalize my thoughts." These expressions, although straightforward, prove to be efficacious in unblocking and activating the throat chakra.

Be completely honest" "Provide a truthful account" "Speak candidly" "Disclose the accurate information" "Reveal the unabridged facts

Ultimately, one of the most effective strategies for restoring balance to an obstructed throat chakra is through honest communication. Authentic statements function as nourishing sustenance for our throat chakra, promoting its optimal well-being with increased ingestion.

Exercises

An effective exercise for this specific area and one that provides immediate relief is the act of gently rolling the head. Assume a posture with an aligned spinal column and direct your gaze to the right, proceed to tilt your head rearwards and execute a rotational motion in a counterclockwise fashion. Approach this task with caution and precision rather than hastily, and repeat the same action in the opposite direction. Additionally, profound alleviation for this chakra can be experienced by indulging in the pleasurable activity of singing. It facilitates the activation of the chakra and concurrently fosters tranquility of the mind.

Foods and Drinks

Plum and blueberry are regarded as highly beneficial for the throat chakra owing to their vibrant hue. The throat chakra as well as the hue of blue each epitomize reliability.

Fruits such as apple, apricot, guava, mango, orange, and pear possess attributes that symbolize trustworthiness, therefore rendering them suitable for the purpose of nourishing the throat chakra. They are deemed reliable due to the frequent occurrence of their ripeness-induced detachment.

Similarly, tangy fruits can be highly beneficial for the throat chakra. The aforementioned fruits encompass kiwi, orange, grapefruit, and lemon. Salt and lemongrass are the most optimal flavor enhancers for this particular chakra.

Lifting the Veil

Your essence, your transcendent being, abides in this place. On earth. You are engaged in the process of a mortal existence. The aforementioned mistakes, failures, and life struggles that you have encountered, at times persevered through, should not be construed as they may initially appear. According to Malcolm Forbes, "Failures can lead to success if we derive valuable lessons from them." Every acquired lesson enhances our proximity to our inner self, further aligning us with our true essence. In a manner akin to the alignment of your chakras, the energy centers within you, the alignment with your soul engenders a state of contentment and vitality in your spiritual essence.

Your elevated self refers to that aspect of your being which possesses an acute understanding, perception, and awareness of the surrounding circumstances, attained through the highest levels of personal growth, while simultaneously being embodied in your human form. However, your soul originates from an alternate dimension, consequently granting it a distinct perspective compared to your human self. Whenever an individual examines a complex scenario from an alternate vantage point and discerns that excessive apprehension is being bestowed upon insignificant matters within the broader context, they are undergoing personal growth. When an individual assimilates a life lesson, undergoes the transformative process, derives learnings from it, and progresses forward, they undergo personal growth and development. Through every encounter, one undergoes personal growth. Don't block the blessings.

On each occasion when you experience a premonition, a sudden surge of intuition, a sensation of uncertain origin, it signifies that your elevated consciousness is endeavoring to communicate a message that it deems imperative for you to comprehend. Your heightened state of consciousness serves as the most invaluable compass to navigate this intricate journey we refer to as human existence.

What factors impede progress? You. More specifically, your ego. You appear to have a multitude of thoughts running through your mind, accompanied by a significant amount of extraneous mental clutter that can be effectively disregarded through practice. Your decisions are greatly influenced by your accumulated knowledge and experiences. Through guidance from parental figures, educators, societal norms, or collective perceptions of right and wrong.

Naturally, you possess an innate understanding of what aligns with your individual needs. You simply lack ample experience in honing your ability to attune to your inner voice. Hence, this is the reason for your presence and the act of perusing this . I am compelled to present to you this intricate correlation which holds an extraordinary magnitude beyond ordinary comprehension. We must foster the growth of that. It's important.

What strategies can be employed to distinguish one's ego from their higher self? This is easy. Your ego aligns itself with sensations of fear, anxiety, tension, and anger. The conscious and persistent entity is the one that acquires knowledge through its experiences. Your sense of self incorporates all the pain, disillusionment, sorrow, and pessimism you have experienced. Hence, the act of bearing that burden can have detrimental consequences. The ego derives satisfaction from a sense of pride, but exhibits aversion towards shame. Your ego experiences intense fear as a result of the mentioned situation, and as a result, it will go to great lengths to shield and safeguard you from it. Shame primarily originates from our apprehension of facing judgment and ridicule. It is a rather uneasy predicament to find oneself in. On each occasion we relinquish attachment to such matters and simply accept our experiences as they are, whether positive, negative, or unfavorable, we can regard the lessons learned as fortuitous concealed advantages. We can grow. That is the purpose for which we are present. As previously mentioned, as it has been reiterated by numerous individuals, it is imperative not to obstruct the occurrence of favorable events.

Let us engage in a brief meditation session for this objective. Cognizance of your elevated self, that crucial bond with your elevated self.

The Silk Cord (with a duration of 15 minutes)

Please locate a suitable area for reclining.

Commence by reclining and gently shutting your eyelids.

I shall commence a countdown, starting from the numerical value of ten. As I commence the process of counting in reverse order, you will gradually experience a palpable release of tension and the expulsion of negative energy from your very being. This energy will permeate the layers of your external covering, descend towards the ground below, and ultimately disperse and dissipate into the surrounding environment.

10..........9...........8

7...........6............5

4..........3.............2

1

Your musculature is in a state of relaxation, commencing from the cranial region and extending downwards to encompass the auditory organs, progressing through your neck and shoulders, ultimately reaching the state of relaxation in your arms and hands.

Experience the sensation of calmness spreading from your chest, abdomen, and extending all the way down to your lower extremities, including your legs and toes.

I now kindly request that you place your left hand delicately and in a state of comfort upon your heart. This represents your current state or condition.

Please position your right hand onto the region where there is a division or opening amidst your rib cage. This represents the essence of your being, encompassing your soul, spirit, and elevated self. Ensure that you are able to maintain a comfortable position with your hands in that location.

Breathe in.

Breathe out.

Inhale slightly more profoundly.

Breathe out.

You are protected, comfortably sheltered, and well-protected.

Breathe in.

Breathe out.

You are assured of your safety, comfort, and protection.

Breathe in.

Breathe out.

You are sheltered, cozy, and protected.

There exists an infinite connection between your physical self and your soul. You both collectively constitute a single individual. An amazing human being.

Infinity

Inhale that idea as you take in that breath.

Breathe out.

Infinity

Inhale deeply, allowing the convergence of your heart and soul to establish a profound connection within you. The existence of one is contingent upon the presence of the other.

Breathe out.

Envision, if you will, a pristine silk cord of white hue, symbolizing vitality and nurturing, delicately entwining itself around your left hand, traversing over your heart, and gracefully looping into a figure-eight pattern around your right hand, encompassing your soul's essence. Gently guide your hands along the pathway of the infinite symbol.

Breathe in.

Breathe out.

As you inhale and exhale, repeatedly visualize tracing the symbol of infinity within the depths of your mind's perception.

With the inhalation, one experiences the sensation of being intricately linked or connected.

As each exhalation escapes, you sense the fortification of that interconnection.

Direct your gaze towards the white silk cord ensconcing your hands, in a pattern reminiscent of the infinite symbol, through the perception of your third eye chakra.

The luminous white silk cord serves as a tangible representation of the profound interdependence between your physical being and your spiritual essence.

Your perceptive third eye chakra discerns the emanation of divine luminescence, manifested as a resplendent white glow, coursing through the intricate network of the cord, traversing the space betwixt your two hands.

Gradually lower your hands, placing them by your sides in a position that is most optimal for your comfort.

Eight: The Restoration of the Fifth Chakra

The Vishuddha chakra, also known as the fifth chakra or throat chakra, is represented by the concept of ether, associated with purity and the essence of the human race. It epitomizes artistic manifestation, our capacity to articulate veracity and foster connections, vision, and discernment. From a physiological standpoint, it is situated in males posterior to the Adam's apple, while in females it is positioned in the exact center of the throat. It is anatomically connected with every occurrence involving the teeth, oral cavity, pharynx, and thyroid glands.

The fifth chakra, which is regarded as the center of vital communication, is intricately linked to our capacity to transcend our physical being. This encompasses various forms of communication such as verbal expressions that impact others, the realm of dreams, experiences beyond our physical form, and the heightened auditory perception known as clairaudience. When the fifth chakra is in a state of equilibrium and functioning optimally, it facilitates a sense of inner balance, contentment, and accountability.

In the event that the fifth chakra is not functioning optimally, it may manifest in the manifestation of various physical ailments such as throat soreness, throat infections, voice impairment, earaches, and any issue linked to the process of communication. Recurrent issues related to this particular chakra are evident in physiological conditions such as thyroid and sinus problems, as well as a pervasive state of weariness and depletion. In exceptionally severe instances, this can culminate in the development of chronic fatigue syndrome and fibromyalgia.

From an emotional standpoint, persistent issues concerning this chakra can render us susceptible to the dominance of others and impede our ability to express our true selves.

Associated fragrances: Benzoin and frankincense

Herbs corresponding to the aforementioned: Eugenia, vervain, and cloves.

Associated glandular system: Thyroid

Musical note: G

Phonetic representation of the chakra sound: The vowel 'E' is pronounced as a short sound, similar to that in words like let, get, and bet.

Element: Ether and earth

Color: Blue

The following gemstones exhibit shades of blue: sapphire, celestite, blue topaz, sodalite, lapis lazuli, aquamarine, azurite, kyanite, chalcedony, turquoise, and chrysocolla.

Healing exercise:

Any form of vocalization or recitation.

Shoulder stands

Healing foods:

Various types of fruit juices"
"Assorted assortments of fruit juices
Juices and teas

Healing the Sixth Chakra

The chakra known as the sixth, or Ajna, is located slightly above the space between the eyebrows, with a prominent association in the realm of parapsychology and mysticism as the "third eye." The sixth chakra symbolizes the manifestation of wisdom and perceptive faculties, as well as the embodiment of the inquisitive intellect. The key quality of this is its profound level of perception, extending to the extent of anticipation, which demonstrates our heightened mental awareness and vigilance.

When the equilibrium of this chakra is maintained, it enables us to delve profoundly into the underlying factors of various phenomena and enhance our abilities of intuition. This refers not to mere 'gut instincts', but rather to our faculties of sixth sense, enabling us to think creatively and draw accurate inferences regarding individuals and circumstances we come across. To external observers, the thoroughly developed and flourishing sixth chakra may seem to border on the supernatural. This is not without justification, as this chakra serves as the passageway to the elevated spiritual planes and contributes to the establishment of our affiliation with the realms of imagination and truth. In the event that the sixth chakra exhibits an excessively rapid rotational motion, accompanied by an augmented size in comparison to the inferior chakras, the individual in question is inclined to preoccupy themselves excessively with fantasies, others, contemplations, and the ethereal dimensions. This preoccupation may engender a state of paranoia, fear, or affliction within said individual.

Indications of deficiencies in this particular chakra encompass cognitive impairment, diminished capacity to concentrate, disturbances during sleep, episodes of head pain, as well as a general dearth of introspection and an inability to perceive those in our vicinity. In contrast to the other chakras, the primary issue associated with the sixth chakra does not lie in its blockage, but rather in its premature or excessive opening. During the practice of chakra balancing, one will gain an understanding of the interconnectedness of the chakras and their integral role in a sequential and incremental progression. Once you have established a sense of safety and security, you are afforded the opportunity to cultivate your connection to enjoyment and contentment. Once you have acquired the ability to attend to your own well-being and address your personal requirements, instruction is provided on the proper strategies for effective communication and establishing connections with fellow individuals. This is the procedure by which each individual chakra progressively unfolds and matures in their inherent sequence, transpiring continuously over the course of our lifetime, but particularly in the early years until the age of 29.

In the event that the premature activation or advancement of the sixth chakra occurs (for instance, in the context of an intense fixation on daydreaming or fantasy, or indulging in substances or psychic practices), the issue lies not in its failure to open, but in its excessive reception of perceptions regarding the astral and subtle domains. Consequently, the remaining chakras and the integration of our mind and body are unable to harmonize fully, as they themselves have not yet attained adequate levels of development.

Five: Therapeutic Techniques for Balancing Chakras

It is quite prevalent for individuals to encounter a diverse range of health issues and even illnesses due to an obstruction in the energetic flow within our chakras. Some examples encompassing the aforementioned are cardiovascular disorders, diminished self-confidence, migraines, gastrointestinal disturbances, weakened immune responses, chronic fatigue, sexual impairments, familial and interpersonal conflicts, diminished creative expression, and perturbed hormonal equilibrium, among others. Nevertheless, one can mitigate and potentially eradicate these issues by actively participating in a range of exercises and techniques specifically crafted to enhance the energy circulation within one's chakras and enhance their overall functionality.

These exercises provide an exceptional means to enhance the function of your chakras, thereby facilitating manifold enhancements in your health and overall well-being. In addition, they possess remarkable therapeutic properties and serve as highly effective stress alleviators, inducing a deep sense of relaxation.

Below is a comprehensive compilation of highly beneficial exercises and techniques tailored to enhance and cultivate the vitality and balance of each unique chakra within an individual's subtle energy system:

1). Root Chakra

Indications of Impaired Chakra Functioning:

Exhaustion, familial conflicts, and disorientation stemming from a loss of stability.

Methods for enhancing the robustness of this particular chakra:

One may enhance the vitality of this chakra through the practice of envisioning a flowing stream of molten lava beneath oneself, or by visualizing the growth of tree roots extending deeply into the earth from one's body and feet. This is due to the fact that the root chakra aligns with the ancestral or genealogical origins of an individual. This chakra can be restored by addressing and processing these underlying emotions.

An additional method that aids in the fortification of your root chakra involves visualizing the vibrant radiance of the color red emanating prominently from the region situated at the foundation of your spine, which is the precise location of your root chakra. Continue by envisioning a crimson light extending downwards through your lower extremities and connecting you firmly to the ground.

2). Sacral Chakra

Indicators of Diminished Chakra Energy: Sexual incapacity, endocrine disruption, diminished imaginative capacity.
Methods to enhance the vitality of this chakra:
The sacral chakra can be enhanced through engaging in any form of creative or affirming sexual expression.

3). Solar Plexus Chakra

"Indicators of Diminished Chakra Resilience:

Gastrointestinal problems, diminished strength in the central musculature, compromised immune function, diminished self-confidence.

"Methods for enhancing the function of this specific chakra:

This energy center can be significantly enhanced through the act of devoting time to introspection and reevaluating personal decisions and life trajectories.

4). Heart Chakra

Indications of Diminished Chakra Functionality:

Elevated or reduced blood pressure, cardiac manifestations, feelings of anger, sensory numbness, apprehension towards affection.

Methods for enhancing the potency of this chakra:

The heart chakra holds significance due to its role as the focal point for one's emotions. To enhance the vitality of this chakra, one must cultivate a disposition that embraces the diverse range of emotions encountered throughout life's myriad experiences. This encompasses aspects such as affection, bereavement, suffering, and delight. One may envision a radiant white light at the core of the chest and permit it to gradually expand. This has the potential to stimulate the heart chakra and alleviate sensations of discomfort. Keeping a record of your thoughts, emotions, and personal encounters within a journal can prove advantageous.

5). Throat Chakra

Indicators of a Diminished Chakra:

Overactive or underactive thyroid, feelings of frustration, fear, or difficulty in verbal communication

Methods for enhancing the vitality of this chakra:
One may enhance the functioning of the throat chakra through activities such as vocalizing, engaging in expressive movement, composing written works, or engaging in articulate discourse. The purification and fortification of this particular chakra can be achieved through the thoughtful articulation of one's authentic truth, the assertion of one's convictions, and the unwavering adherence to personal beliefs.

6). Third Eye Chakra

Indicators of a Depleted Chakra Energy Flow:
Symptoms include migraines, diminished cognitive clarity, and a sense of disorientation.
Methods for enhancing the energetic prowess of this particular chakra:

One may assist in purifying and fortifying the third eye (or brow) chakra through the act of envisioning a third eye situated in the center of the forehead, engaging in astutely perceptive and insightful observation. Excessive rumination can lead to fatigue and hinder the activity of the brow chakra. Therefore, it is advisable to allocate moments for meditation, in which the mind can experience respite from ceaseless contemplation. This method is indeed exemplary in enhancing the vitality of the third eye chakra.

7). Crown Chakra

Indicators of Diminished Chakra Potential:
Indicators of a compromised crown chakra encompass symptoms such as migraines, cognitive impairment,

apprehension, alienation or dissociation, skepticism, and a dearth of confidence, optimism, and belief.

Here are techniques to enhance the vitality of this particular chakra:

The crown chakra symbolizes our profound and innate link with the celestial realms. Imagine a radiant sphere of luminous white energy descending and encircling your head, gently unfolding and restoring harmony to the crown chakra. Descend this energy and envelop your physical form as a safeguarding barrier. Engaging in vocal communication with a celestial entity such as God or a guardian angel can significantly enhance and invigorate the energy of the crown chakra.

FIVE
YOGA: THE APPLICATION OF MINDFUL RESPIRATION

B

Respiration is a vital aspect of yoga practice. We respire in an automated and subconscious manner, assimilating the essential oxygen necessary for our survival while simultaneously excreting carbon dioxide. There exist multiple methods of respiration.

Abdominal respiration: primarily involves breathing through the abdominal region.

The costal breathing: primarily occurs within the thoracic region.

Supraclavicular respiration or superior respiration.

Yoga and other modalities of wellness employ intentional breathing techniques that yield various advantageous outcomes for both the physical and mental state.

The Art of Pranayama: Mastering Breath Control in the Discipline of Yoga

Yoga considers the act of breathing to be fundamental to its core tenets.

Yoga exercises consistently incorporate the practice of controlled breathing. Each exercise is accentuated by the act of breathing, specifically utilizing nasal inhalation instead of oral respiration.

It is customary to commence by initiating an exhalation in order to fully exhale and rid the lungs of any surplus air. Respiration plays a crucial role in facilitating the flow of essential energy and consequently holds tremendous significance in maintaining equilibrium in energy levels.

Pranayama is a term derived from the Sanskrit language:

\\\"Prana\\\" means energy,

\\\"Ayama\\\" refers to vitality.

The Advantages of Proper Breathing in the Practice of Yoga

The act of relaxation is frequently achieved through intentional breath control, focusing on the abdomen. By assuming a supine position and employing deep inhalations and exhalations, individuals can effectively induce a state of relaxation. This can be facilitated by placing one's hands on the abdomen and attentively directing attention towards the rhythm of inhalation and exhalation.

It is crucial to inhale deeply and avoid shallow breathing.

Adequate respiration is imperative for both physiological and psychological well-being.

The advantageous effects of yoga and controlled breathing techniques on the physiological realm

Rids the body of harmful substances," "Removes toxins from the system," "Purges the body of toxins," "Expels harmful substances from the body.

Improves blood circulation,

Slows the heart rate,
Lowers blood pressure,
Regenerates the body,
Relaxes the body,
Promotes healing
On the mental plane

Facilitates a state of mental tranquility and enhanced clarity,
Facilitates the development of stronger self-assurance.
Facilitates problem-solving
Facilitates enhanced focus and improved memory retention.
Emotionally, it enables the liberation from nervous tensions and other related issues.
Various forms of yogic respiration
"Diverse categories of yogic breathwork"
"Various styles of pranayama in yoga"
In yoga classes, there are various forms of breath control techniques that are

commonly instructed. Among these breaths:

Integrated respiration: encompassing the coordinated activation of abdominal, costal, and clavicular breathing, facilitating the comprehensive movement of air within the respiratory system, extending up to the cranial region.
Solar respiration
clean breathing
Alternate breathing, etc.
The acquisition of knowledge regarding yoga and breath control techniques is imperative.
Engaging in yoga exercises with inadequate or improper breathing yields no benefit.
Prior to embarking on independent practice, acquiring the guidance of a competent instructor is of utmost importance. This particular exercise is

designed to rectify our imperfections, both in terms of the physical activity and our approach to proper breathing techniques.

For individuals who experience inadequate respiration, engaging in yoga exercises would facilitate their development of mindfulness towards their breathing patterns.

CONSEQUENCES OF BAD BREATHING

When one is beset by overpowering emotions or experiences high levels of stress or anxiety, a respiratory response occurs, known as 'dyspnea' or 'respiratory distress'. Inadequate respiration may significantly impact our overall state, culminating in:

Nervous and physical fatigue,
Poor resistance to stress,
Digestive problems,
Palpitations,
Lack of concentration, etc.

CONNECTION OF THE CHAKRAS

There are a total of seven chakras, and it is worth noting that the five chakras positioned in the middle have corresponding kshetras. The seven chakras can be perceived and interlinked within the framework of the five chakras, commonly referred to as the microcosmic or macrocosmic cycle.

The phenomenon of microcosmic circulation encompasses the circulation pathway starting at the apex of the forehead, moving through the throat, heart, abdomen, pubic area, and genitals, extending to the pelvic floor region, then reversing the path upon exhalation and proceeding towards the sacrum, lumbar spine, thoracic spine, cervical spine, and concluding at the back of the head.

The connection with exhalation can be established by inhaling towards the front and exhaling towards the upper back region. In the Ujjayi meditation practice, the technique is consistently followed, either through the microcosmic cycle or the macrocosmic cycle. During the inhalation phase, one directs their attention downward towards the depths of the earth, pausing briefly to connect with the earth's energy. On the exhalation, the focus shifts upwards along the spine towards the expansive expanse of the sky, pausing once more to attune to the vastness above. Inhaling from the celestial realm to the earthly depths, one maintains a connection with the terrestrial plane and exhales through the sushumna and crown chakra.

The downward flow of energy from above is occasionally denoted and favorably known as Saraswati Nadi at Yoga Vidya. Saraswati Nadi holds alternative designations in various nomenclatures.

Sushumna is the energetic pathway that ascends from the lower region of the body up towards the spine. Hence, one may engage in what is commonly referred to as the sushumna activation breath, wherein the breath is directed from the frontal region to the center of the forehead, and then further down through the sushumna channel towards the muladhara chakra. Upon reaching the muladhara, one proceeds to exhale along the sushumna, directing the breath towards the middle of the head, situated forward over the forehead.

Certain individuals opt to invigorate their breath, while others prefer directing their attention towards the Sahasrara chakra. Additionally, there are those who derive pleasure from generating either microcosmic or macrocosmic circulation in the heart, or alternatively, within the vicinity of the head. This is done in order to induce a state of complete tranquility.

Four: Acoustic Phenomena and Oscillatory Motions

The entirety of the cosmos, including each and every particle and subatomic structure, is comprised of oscillations.

The utilization of sound and the recitation of mantras for the purpose of healing generate vibrations that serve to diminish stress, modify one's state of consciousness, and foster a profound sense of tranquility, overall wellness, and physical well-being. There exists a state of harmonic resonance, a sonic therapy aimed at restoring equilibrium within your physical, emotional, and spiritual essence.

Scientific evidence has demonstrated the efficacy of sound healing in the treatment of cancer patients, leading to decreased levels of stress and improved pain management. Mantras possess the transcendent healing frequencies inherent in the cosmic realm. Individuals have the option to engage in the recitation or contemplation of mantras. They function as a tool for the dissolution of the egoic mind and the elevation of spiritual awareness.

Mantras represent the epitome of linguistic expression, embodying the pinnacle of sound in its transcendent state, as they enable us to transcend egocentric tendencies, self-serving emotions, and excessive self-absorption. When the transcendent sound, often referred to as 'naad' in Hindu philosophy, assumes dominion, it elevates us beyond all other forms of being. This sound has the power to instigate transformative shifts in the global paradigm, bringing about profound transformations in individual lives, communication, and thoughts. It metamorphoses us into entirely novel entities.

Do words generate vibrational patterns, or does the uttered sound dissipate and cease to exist? When we engage in the practice of reciting mantras, what is the destination or trajectory of the sound vibrations? Were you aware of the fact that sounds possess visual representations? The radiance encountered during the recitation of mantras originates from the resonance of an elevated frequency that influences the cerebral function but remains largely forgotten in the state of ordinary awareness. This experience is also associated with the heart lotus and represented by the image of a rapidly moving antelope, indicating that it is fleeting, eluding comprehension before the mind can fully capture it.

Frequently, a significant duration of time is required before our intellect grants us entry into that concealed realm, which is inaccessible to our ordinary waking awareness. With diligent and uninterrupted practice, the mantra will ultimately take root within us and manifest its true essence. However, attaining this state necessitates steadfast commitment and the absence of any influence stemming from the egoic mind.

The material world, perceptible through the five senses, should not be mistaken for true reality, but rather regarded as a construct. It is necessary to eliminate all adverse mental imprints prior to cultivating positive ones, which can be achieved through consistent engagement in meditation and recitation of mantras.

Techniques for Restoring Balance

There are several different methods that are actively used today to restore an imbalanced chakra, or chakras, back into perfect balance. This will discuss the different methods that are most commonly used to restore balance to the chakras, how you can tap into your chakras yourself, exercise them, and their abilities, as well as some practices that you can adopt into your daily lifestyle so that you will be able to better keep all of your chakras in balance from this point on.

There are several different types of meditation that an individual can use to restore balance to every aspect of their being. I will first go over the forms of meditation that are most well known and explain how they are used. They are Mindfulness Meditation, Zazen, Transcendental Meditation, Kundalini, Heart-rhythm, and guided visualization. Out of these few, the only specific one that is used to help exercise the chakras is Kundalini. I am mentioning all of these, though because I strongly feel that doing some form of meditation, even if it is not directly related to the chakras or balancing that energy, is much better than nothing and will work to improve your health in various ways. After we go through these basic forms of meditation, we will go more into depth on how to balance the chakras.

Mindfulness meditation, sometimes also referred to as Vipassana, comes from Buddhist traditions. This is the most popular form of meditation in western world. This form of meditation is based on becoming more aware of your breath and detaching from your thoughts. When practicing, the individual should not try to limit the thoughts they have, but rather, they should practice detaching, or letting go of each one as they come into the mind. A person should also not try to control their breathing, they should just become more aware of their breathing pattern.

Zazen, which is known by most people as "Zen", is another form of meditation that comes from Buddhist traditions. When most people think of this form of meditation, they think of it as just sitting and relaxing. This is because it is done in a sitting position, using correct posture (your back is kept straight and head facing forward) for long periods of time. The time periods are often long because this form of meditation was originally developed for a monastic setting. Although the lengthy involvement of this meditation can seem very challenging to study, it requires little to no guidance.

Transcendental meditation is very similar to Zen meditation, except it comes from Hindu traditions. For this form, a person is also sitting in a Lotus (define) or half-Lotus (define) posture and is able to focus on their breathing patterns. However, rather than trying to detach from thoughts as they come into the mind, a particular word is chosen and is mentally repeated over and over. The goal is that the individual will rise above everything that is temporal (or temporary, physical) and be able to eventually enter into an out of body experience.

Kundalini is another form of meditation that comes from Hindu traditions. This form may be one of the most important ones when it comes to balancing chakras because the person's breathing actually has an impact on where their energy is within their body. While using this form of meditation, the individual is attempting to become more aware of the stream of energy that exists within the chakras. Awareness of your breathing is, of course, important with this form of meditation, just like in all the others we have covered before this. With this form, being aware of your breathing patterns is even more important, though, because it is strongly believed that each breath is to be used to move all of the energy upwards, through the body and to the top of the head, to the crown chakra.

While practicing heart-rhythm meditation, the individual's main focus is on breathing and the heartbeat. The goal with this form of meditation is for the person to be able to achieve a complete balance between both their breathing and their heartbeat. While meditating, the individual focuses on identifying themselves with their heart and striving to make their heart the very center of their energetic system. Practicing this form of meditation will help the individual to be better able to increase their sensitivity, compassion, and inner power.

Guided visualization is a very popular form of meditation in the western world. It does not have any roots in any spiritual traditions. Most often, when practicing this form of meditation, an individual will use recorded tapes to guide them through an experience. Sometimes they are looking at a picture of something while listening to the recording and imagining the experience taking place, but photographs are not necessary, and some people find that they are able to focus better with their eyes closed. Some examples of the experiences that the tapes might guide them through are walking through a path in the woods or sitting and relaxing on a beach. This guided imagery, combined with slow, relaxed breathing, has been proven to be very effective at relaxing the muscles and decreasing anxiety. It can also help with work performance (as can all of the other forms of meditation we have talked about) because a large amount of concentration is involved, therefore, the more time one spends practicing any form of meditation, the more their ability to concentrate will improve over time.

www.ingramcontent.com/pod-product-compliance
Lightning Source LLC
Chambersburg PA
CBHW050416120526
44590CB00015B/1991